John Baptist De La Salle

Patron of Teachers

by
J.B. Midgley

All booklets are published thanks to the generous support of the members of the Catholic Truth Society

CATHOLIC TRUTH SOCIETY
PUBLISHERS TO THE HOLY SEE

Contents

Foreword

Bishop Patrick O'Donoghue of Lancaster published a significant educational text, *Fit for Mission? Schools* (CTS, 2008), in which he encouraged Catholic education establishments to renew the fire of faith in an authentic Catholic ethos, avail themselves of the corporate experience of teachers, parents, and clergy, and regard the *Catechism of the Catholic Church* as an invaluable resource. In his kindness, God presents every age with holy men and women to refresh his pilgrim people, and the Holy Spirit breathes new life into human endeavour. In the timely context offered by Bishop O'Donoghue there is an illustrious advocate in heaven whose charity and powerful intercession does not diminish with the passing of time.

In the seventeenth century, John Baptist De La Salle renounced wealth, and the probability of an eminent ecclesiastical career, to devote himself to the education of youth. He recognised that children must be equipped with skills for life so that they can play their important role in the Church's continuing mission, and receive the education of mind and spirit to enjoy the fruits of salvation in the kingdom of heaven. He therefore asked teachers to value their profession "as one of the most excellent in the Church, for it is one most suited to sustain it and give it a solid foundation." He loved his own vocation as priest and educator and, like Saint Ignatius of Loyola, taught other subjects so that he would "have the right to teach Christian doctrine, to understand God's goodness in creating us, and meet his wish that we all come to know the truth, and his call to teachers to bring to children the truth of the Gospel."

John's creative response to needs and conditions has contemporary relevance. He recognised that the underprivileged were deprived of social mobility, and valued education as the means of release from poverty and moral despair. He demonstrated that true innovation is capable of implementation by practitioners, and inspires confidence through an evident improvement on what is replaced. He treasured the rich heritage received from the Apostles that stands the test of time. "Hold fast to what is of faith," he advised. "Shun novelties, follow the traditions of the Church, receive only what she receives, condemn only what she condemns, approve what she approves. In all things render her prompt obedience."

History acclaims him as the father of modern pedagogy whose classroom methodology was a pattern for succeeding generations, and as a philosopher whose treatises on education have become classics. He pioneered the provision of elementary, technical, and special schools, training colleges for secular and religious teachers, adult and higher education and, most of all, founded a unique, religious teaching order, the Institute of the Brothers of the Christian Schools. Gratitude must be expressed to a distinguished member, Brother Thomas Campbell, FSC, for his invaluable guidance and generous assistance in preparing this tribute to a great saint.

Downham Market, October 2008

Early Years and Priesthood

In 1555, the Catholic German empire accepted the legality of the Protestant religion at the Peace of Augsburg. Unfortunately, hostilities resumed in 1618 when Bohemian nobles threw two of Emperor Ferdinand's regents out of a fatally high window in Prague. Ferdinand declared war on Frederick V, the Protestant king of Bohemia and, with the help of Philip III of Spain, seized the estates of Protestants in Bohemia, Austria and Moravia, and closed their churches and schools. The conflict engulfed Europe as rulers in north Germany and Denmark tried to reclaim lost territories with the help of English and Dutch forces. Ferdinand's imperial and Catholic armies defeated them and, in 1629, he decreed that Protestants must restore Catholic properties they had seized. In 1648, just three years before John was born, the Peace of Westphalia confirmed the Augsburg agreement, and gave legal recognition to individual freedom of worship and belief. However, the influence of the Holy Roman Empire ended, and the modern secularisation of international relations began. The English Civil War was coming to an end, and Cromwell was inflicting terrible punishment on Irish Catholics for supporting the Royalist cause.

An uneasy peace did not restore equilibrium in France. Louis XIV's reign (1638-1715) witnessed a surge in Gallicanism, as secular and clerical efforts were made to release the national Church from what was considered intrusive Roman control. Lavish expenditure in high places and privileges for the powerful widened the gap between rich and poor, especially in the city slums and rural areas. "Wars of Religion" had brought untold suffering, with families broken by the loss of husbands and fathers, the plundering of crops by rampaging military, and consequent famine. False doctrines undermined faith and stifled conscience, and what few schools existed were poorly attended. Ignorance was rampant, and children were increasingly left to their own devices, growing up deprived of guidance or hope for the future.

The family

The De La Salle family originates in the early years of the ninth century with Johan Salla who was the Commander in Chief of the Spanish Royal forces of King Alonso the Chaste. About 1350, the junior branch moved to France and settled in Champagne where, three centuries later, John entered the world in Reims on 30th April 1651. He was the first of eleven children born to Louis De La Salle, a prosperous lawyer, and Nicole Moet whose name still survives in the Moet et Chandon brand of champagne. Louis and Nicole were devoted parents who engaged a private tutor for their children and did all they could to ensure their intellectual and moral development. Nicole's parents who shared the splendid home, L'Hôtel de la Cloche, also took a benign and supportive interest, especially in John who would succeed his father as head of the family.

Saint Vincent de Paul died in 1660. He was revered by clergy, laity, rich, poor, outcasts and convicts, all of whom had experienced the goodness of one selflessly consumed by love of God and love of neighbour. All France mourned, especially the people of Paris where his sanctity and care for the poor was legendary. His work, influence and skill had effected a change in social consciousness that would benefit Europe and the wider world. The citizens of Reims had a poignant reason to share this grief because the money he raised and sent regularly had alleviated the suffering of the poor during the religious conflicts. A commemoration Mass was celebrated in the Cathedral and, undoubtedly, the De La Salle family would have been present. Perhaps the seed of another fruitful apostolate was sown as John, aged nine, heard the story of Vincent's wonderful achievements. Certainly, a benign Providence was arranging that as Vincent's life ended, a new champion of the poor was about to emerge.

The young student

That same year, John began his formal education at the nearby Collège des Bons Enfants where he would spend seven years before normal admission to Reims University. Every subject was taught in Latin and the texts and methodology were uninspiring, but he applied himself conscientiously and made excellent progress. His grandmother shared her interest in the lives of the saints with him, and his grandfather, who recited the Divine Office every day, introduced him to the Psalms that were the prayers of our Lord himself. When he was eleven, John expressed an interest in becoming a priest, to the initial consternation of his father who hoped a brilliant career as a lawyer in the family tradition lay ahead. However, Louis and Nicole arranged for him to receive the tonsure, the first minor order that did not necessarily commit him to the clerical life, but made him eligible for ecclesiastical benefits.

Canon of Reims

John's uncle, Canon Pierre Dozet, was chancellor of Reims University and presiding officer of academic sessions. He was so impressed by his nephew's qualities that when he decided to resign his canonry in 1666, he nominated him as his successor. On 7th January 1667, John was solemnly installed as a Canon of the Metropolitan See of Reims at the tender age of sixteen. The duties were not demanding and, as soon as he entered university, his only responsibility was to assist at High Mass four times a year.

Saint-Sulpice

John graduated as a Master of Arts of the University of
Reims on 10th July 1669. A year later he entered the
Seminary of Saint-Sulpice to study for the priesthood,
and it is worth reflecting on an establishment that was to
have a lasting influence.

In 1641, Father Jean Jaques Olier, the parish priest of
Saint-Sulpice in Paris, had gathered together a group of
clergy who shared his dedication to the spiritual and
intellectual formation of aspirants to the priesthood. They
lived as a community in a house attached to the church of
Saint Sulpicius (Sulpicius was a beloved seventh century
Bishop of Bourges), where they opened the first seminary
under his patronage. The French School of Spirituality
initiated by Cardinal Pierre de Berulle was distinguished
by the greatest reverence for Our Lady, the Mother of God,
so it was natural that she should be revered as Patroness of
the seminary where "a most filial confidence and tender
devotion were the characteristics of the house." The
Society became identified with the reform of seminary
education, and the continuing supportive development of
the clergy through prayer, spiritual conference and study
with consequent benefit to parish life.

Father Olier wanted his seminarians to be holy,
cultured, and expert in the knowledge needed for their
incomparable mission, and he arranged that they should

attend courses at the University of the Sorbonne, then a stronghold of uncontaminated faith and a bastion against Jansenism. Bishop Cornelius Jansen of Ypres (1585-1638) had written a treatise, *Augustinus,* that distorted Saint Augustine's teaching by advocating a rigorous spirituality to stifle human nature that he regarded as essentially corrupt. In assessing grace and free will, he followed Protestant thinking that grace was so irresistible that free will was insignificant, and its sufficiency made good works superfluous. Despite the promotion of a severe morality, and the chances of salvation viewed with pessimism, Jansenism attracted a strong following. Pope Innocent X's condemnation in 1653 was seen by the French as an affront to their independent integrity and, in the ensuing tension, a national movement with theological overtones asserted that Papal authority should be exercised only with the approval of a General Council.

Children's Catechism

In seventeenth century France, as elsewhere, education was considered inappropriate, even undesirable, for the working-class poor, but the Sulpicians regarded themselves as educators as well as guardians of souls. Successive superiors of Saint-Sulpice, aware of the dangers that awaited children growing up in ignorance, conducted charity schools as well as running a large parish and a seminary. Father Olier believed that "God's plan for the reform of the Church was to secure the young by teaching them Christian principles and inculcating the fundamental maxims of salvation." On Sundays, major feasts, and in preparation for First Holy Communion and Confirmation, one group of seminarians would go through the streets ringing a hand bell to summon the children of the parish, while another gave instruction.

One of Father Olier's successors regretted the lack of enthusiasm on the part of the clergy. "Regarding children's catechism, only slight effort is brought to this work, no preparation is made, no methods of encouragement such as the distribution of pictures used, no expense ever deemed worthwhile, no arrangement for the children to sit comfortably, nor the place and time well chosen. The children are not sought out from house to house and encouraged to come, nor are their names put on record." John's experience at Saint-Sulpice kept the importance of catechism in the forefront of his mind, and in the objectives of the religious institute he would found.

Sorbonne

Meanwhile at the Sorbonne, John's progress was outstanding. He was fortunate in having the direction of Louis Tronson, another native of Reims who was renowned as a distinguished writer of the French school of spirituality, and for his scholarship and teaching expertise in theology, sacred Scripture, the history of the Church, and the teaching of the Fathers. His Superior wrote of a model Sulpician, "John distinguished himself by the vigour of his intellectual progress and understanding of theology. He was a constant observer of the Rule. His conversation was always pleasing and above reproach. He never offended anyone, nor incurred criticism."

The Theology doctorate course at the Sorbonne was designed to last nine years. John had completed only nine months when his mother, Nicole who was only thirty-six, died on 19th July 1671. Eight months later, Louis followed his wife to the grave so, at twenty-one, John found himself head of the family and responsible for the education and welfare of his siblings. Though devastated to leave Saint-Sulpice, he devoted himself wholeheartedly to his new responsibilities, supervising the education of his brothers and sisters with discretion, administrative flair, and a gentle touch in human relationships. This was at personal cost and his biographer, Canon Blain, records the mental anguish that he valiantly resolved by prayer, and with help from Canon Nicholas Roland, a theologian of great spiritual discernment.

Ordination

Thanks to Roland's wise guidance, John was ordained subdeacon by Archbishop Jonnart at Cambrai on 2nd June 1672. For the next four years, he combined the duties of family guardian, his canonry, university studies and, if this were not enough, undertook a host of charitable initiatives directed by his mentor. When he was ordained deacon by

Bishop Batailler of Bethlehem in Paris on 21st March 1676, Roland suggested that the lucrative canonry was hardly compatible with a young cleric's energetic zeal. John immediately asked Archbishop Le Tellier of Reims if he might resign this office and concentrate on preparing for parish work, but permission was not forthcoming. He accepted the decision in obedience, continued as before, and made final preparations for ordination to the priesthood that the Archbishop conducted in Reims Cathedral on Holy Saturday, 9th April 1678. The joy of receiving Holy Orders was marred by sadness at Canon Roland's sudden death two weeks later.

His character

Only illness ever prevented John's daily celebration of Mass, and people were attracted by a piety that was never sanctimonious. A sacristan testified to his fervour, "I was in the sacristy one morning when he entered after Mass. He was so absorbed and enraptured that he could not take off his vestments for a quarter of an hour. I did not disturb him for fear of interrupting his intimate conversation with God." Canon Blain and other contemporaries say that he was above average height, well built, with regular features and blue eyes that shone with intelligence in a face that was agreeably cheerful and calm. He had a quiet air of authority, but was affable and considerate to everyone, and sympathetic to the foibles of others to the extent that his eagerness to forgive was sometimes criticised. People who came to him for advice, always found him approachable, considerate and responsive. His devotion was so evident that it inspired emulation, and many placed themselves under his spiritual direction.

Charity is the distinguishing mark of the Christian, and John radiated God's love. He was invariably kind and patient to those who erred, and gentle in the confessional where he was attentive and generous with his time. He maintained, "It is not enough to have love for our neighbour in our hearts; we must demonstrate it according to his needs and our capability. As Saint John says in his first epistle, 'if we truly love our neighbour, we should show something of the love of Jesus Christ, even to laying down our life for his material and spiritual welfare.'" These are the words of a saint, and John's life is full of examples that justify his right to say them.

Among the clergy in Reims were some powerful Jansenists who tried to win John to their cause. He kept their advances at bay with characteristic charity and courtesy, but this did not avert the animosity that followed their disappointment. He strenuously opposed Jansenism to the end of his life and in every other circumstance was a fearless champion of the faith and the traditional doctrines of the Church. Even when the relationship between the Church in France and Rome was strained, he demonstrated unshakeable loyalty to the See of Peter and felt honoured to sign himself "Roman Priest".

Enlightened Educator

Before his death, Nicholas Roland had entrusted John with the care of the Congregation of the Sisters of the Child Jesus that he had founded to provide free education to girls who lived in poverty. "Your zeal," he said, "will bring it to prosperity and complete the work I have begun. In all this, your model and guide will be Father Nicholas Barré." This saintly priest in Rouen had tried to found an Institute of the "Brothers of the Child Jesus" to teach poor boys but, when the attempt failed, helped Roland establish the Sisters, and open an orphanage. With diplomatic efficiency, John negotiated with Church and civic authorities for the Sisters to be officially recognised, and they were granted authorisation with letters patent in 1679.

Charity to poor schoolteachers

In March that year, his cousin Madame de Maillefer introduced him to Adrien Nyel who had opened four free schools for boys in Rouen and another in Darnetal. She wanted to open another in Reims for which she would pay the schoolmaster's salary, and asked John to help. He did not hesitate and within a month a young man had been appointed, and the first pupils admitted. It is a measure of John's charm that he persuaded Father

Dorigny, parish priest of Saint-Maurice to accommodate both school and teacher in his presbytery. Another charitable lady in the neighbouring parish of Saint-Jaques offered to fund a similar enterprise if John would organise it, which he did with perceptive attention to detail. He then left Adrien Nyel to care for both schools, and quietly withdrew as if this were not his mission.

Pupils flocked to the schools and soon Father Dorigny had six teachers in the presbytery. When finance was inadequate, John made good the difference from his own pocket and found himself increasingly involved. Nyel was now in charge of seven schools but, though his enthusiastic dedication was admirable, his habit of planning another school as soon as one opened created problems. John knew that the remuneration of teaching posts was so pitiful that it did not attract qualified people and, while those appointed could read, they could not necessarily write or calculate. He found himself cast in the role of facilitator, making daily visits, to encourage, suggest practical ways of achieving results, and sharpen a focus on progress and stability. When things went well, he always gave the credit to Nyel.

Unfortunately, by Christmas 1679, Father Dorigny could stand it no longer and asked his guests to find alternative accommodation. John rented a house near his own L'Hôtel de la Cloche and settled them there under the supervision of Nyel who immediately opened yet another school on the premises. John graduated as Doctor of Theology in June 1680 and, with his enviable personal attributes, seemed destined for eminence in the Church, perhaps even to the episcopacy and beyond. He was rich, had no parish duties, his brothers and sisters were less dependent, and his duties as Canon were not burdensome. However, God had other plans and reminded him that he was now personally associated with three struggling schools with inexperienced staff, and that criticism from sceptics was growing.

Birth of the Institute

John went to Paris to consult Father Barré who made the startling suggestion that he take the teachers into his own home where he could train them. John acted on this advice, but caused such a furore in the family that he had to move with them to another rented house in the rue Neuve, leaving L'Hôtel de la Cloche to his brothers and sisters. This momentous day of 24th June 1682, the feast of his patron Saint John the Baptist, can be regarded as the birthday of the Institute of the Brothers of the Christian Schools. Years later, John confessed with whimsical irony, "If I had ever thought that what I did out of charity for poor schoolteachers would mean having to live with them, I would have given up at once."

In consultation with his little community, he drew up a timetable of prayer, daily Mass, meals, teaching hours, study, and essential recreation. Under his benign guidance, their confidence grew, performance blossomed, and public admiration returned with increased demand for their services. New schools in Laon and Rethel were added to Nyel's list, and John looked after those in Reims, but they all became his responsibility when Nyel retired a year later and, little by little, his inevitable mission was revealed.

In the hands of providence

It was understandable that the teachers were worried about the possible impact of an uncertain future on income and conditions of service. They were not entirely convinced when John counselled them to entrust the future to God, and pointed out that he enjoyed the security of wealth and status. He sympathised with them, and again spoke to Father Barré who told him to resign his canonry, give up his fortune, and place himself and the community in God's hands. John hesitated, thinking that his resources and stipend could support the schools and the teachers whose income he already supplemented, but Barré insisted that the work must be founded exclusively on the support of divine Providence. In 1683, John resigned his canonry and a co-incidental famine gave him opportunity to distribute all his worldly goods to the poor. Like his teachers, he was now totally dependent on meagre grants from the schools' patrons. When friends and relatives remonstrated, he answered gently and with certainty, "I must do God's work and, if the worst should come to pass, we shall have to beg for alms."

A new religious order

John came to the conclusion that the survival, growth, and permanence of the schools would best be served if his group became a religious community. He invited twelve of his most promising teachers to join him in retreat, at the end of which they decided to form a congregation called the Brothers of the Christian Schools. On 28th May 1684, before the Blessed Sacrament in the community chapel, they pronounced a simple vow of obedience for one year that could later be a perpetual profession for life. The next day, they walked seventeen miles to Our Lady's shrine at Liesse to place their "Institute" under her protection. For the time being, they followed the timetable and customs of the rue Neuve as the first stage in the development of a Rule that reflected John's confidence in monastic tradition as the support of the active apostolate.

Like other founders, John believed that a distinctive religious habit would indicate that they were in the world but not of it. A black robe with a collar of two linen bands similar to the dress of clergy and lawyers was chosen, with a loose sleeved cloak for protection against the weather. His family were horrified and thought he looked ridiculous walking to school with his Brothers through the streets of Reims in this strange garb. When the Archbishop ordered him to resume conventional clerical dress, John felt obliged to obey.

School life

De La Salle schools were characterised by developments ahead of their time that others would emulate. An early start to the school day was made at 7:15am and the pupils brought their breakfast to eat in school. This provided an opportunity to teach good manners, and encourage kindness towards the needy by contributing to a basket circulated for offerings before Grace was said. The Brothers taught the children the truths of faith, and started every morning session with a reflection on an aspect of Christian life. At mid-day, all sang a hymn before a half hour lesson on Christian doctrine that was followed by the celebration of Mass. The afternoon periods concluded with another hymn and an examination of conscience.

Innovations

John brought enlightened and efficient common sense to the delivery of the secular curriculum of reading, writing and numeracy. He assessed the common practice of teaching through Latin as a barrier to comprehension, so the vehicle for children's learning in his schools was French - the mother tongue. In other educational establishments for what they were worth, children were taught individually, but he introduced the "simultaneous method" of teaching a whole class together. He released the least able from Latin altogether and, as soon as possible, considered age, aptitude, and ability when arranging the composition of classes, an early "setting according to ability and within subjects" that today has found cyclical educational favour. As the years passed and opportunity offered, the curriculum was broadened to the sciences, arts, humanities, and practical skills without any invidious distinction made between academic and vocational courses.

God gives the increase

The brevity of this narrative and the extraordinary rate of achievement must not obscure the difficulties and suffering John endured, and the heroic sacrifices he made. There was public opposition to the fundamental change and development he was implementing, though this eventually melted when his wisdom and expertise had to be acknowledged. The schools, of necessity housed in private dwellings, lacked basic amenities, the crowded rooms were stifling in summer and cold in winter and, since many children were unwashed, the atmosphere was hardly fragrant. Teachers recruited by Adrien Nyel who were not attracted to the religious life left to find alternative employment, and even some of the first twelve members did not renew their vow and left at the end of the first year.

Despite all this, God blessed John's work and others were attracted by his obvious sanctity and enlightened dedication to the education of the poor. Among them were teenagers from good homes, but too young to join the religious community. For them he opened a Junior Novitiate in 1685 and appointed a wise and competent Brother to direct their early preparation for the religious life.

Teacher training

As the Institute's reputation flourished, parish priests elsewhere in the diocese asked John to open schools where none existed, or appoint staff to those that did. A feature of his charism of grace and authority was his inspired readiness to respond to needs as they arose. However, such was the importance he attached to community life that he was reluctant to send a Brother to a rural school that required only one teacher, or to one that was not within walking distance. His solution was to invite the parish priests to send him suitable young men whom his Brothers would train in their method, and equip them as teachers for their parishes. In 1687, he set aside a section of the house in the rue Neuve as the first Training College directed by the Brothers.

School opened in Paris

In 1688, the parish priest of Saint-Sulpice (Paris) asked John if he would take responsibility for a charity school that Father Olier had opened for poor children. Archbishop Le Tellier was not happy when he heard of this because he wanted to keep the Brothers in the Reims diocese, but John saw the advantages the capital offered as a location from which to expand the work of the Institute. On 24th February, he and two Brothers made the long journey to Paris on foot.

Rue Princesse

Saint-Sulpice was one of the poorest areas of the city, but offered a warm and cooperative welcome. A spacious house in the rue Princesse was made available, with large ground floor rooms where classes could be taught, and adequate community accommodation upstairs. Unfortunately, the existing school was disorganised, the pupils unruly, and John had to contend with the jealous mischief-making of the former manager, M. Compagnon, who had the ear of the parish priest. It was a blessing that one of John's old friends, Father Baudrand, became the new incumbent and, with his support, they transformed the school to the delight of parish and parents. In 1690, a second school was opened in the rue du Bac, and two more Brothers joined the rue Princesse community. Further expansion in the capital was rapid, and the Brothers became a familiar sight in their religious habit that John himself would again wear instead of his clerical soutane when going to school to substitute for a teacher who might be ill.

Litigation

Development was not without tribulation. This came from the fee-paying, one teacher establishments known as the Little Schools. The post-holders were alarmed by the number of children attending the Brothers' free schools that were financed by the parish or some other agency. They were particularly upset that payment was not exacted from those who could afford, so that those who could not afford to pay would never be embarrassed. They took their complaints to the Church official responsible for the fee-paying organisation who acted precipitately, raided the premises in the rue du Bac, seized all the furniture, and ordered the school's closure. Despite his legal background, John detested lawsuits which he considered an assault on charity, but he had no option but to seek redress and eventually won his day in court. It was sad that further opposition came from other Church officials who saw vested interests threatened by the Brother's success and popularity, and John had to contend with more lawsuits, court appearances, seizure of schools, and the defection of some disciples.

An Order of Brothers

Following Saint Benedict's example, John intended that some of his congregation should be priests who would say Mass and minister to individual communities. In the first instance, he selected Henri L'Heureux, a young, gifted and holy Brother to study theology at the Sorbonne, and hoped that he would be a future Superior General. Henri completed the course with distinction but on the eve of ordination fell sick and died. This was a shattering blow but as always in time of great sorrow and crisis, John's reaction was to spend the night in prayer, and God granted him comfort, strength, and a new perception of the Institute's purpose. In most religious orders there were both Brothers and priests, but he now determined that his should be composed only of Brothers.

A foundation in which no member, not even the Superior General, would be in Holy Orders was an innovation in the Church. John explained that the Brothers were called to be "Christ's ambassadors to the souls of the young … to pass on the faith and be steeped in it themselves, as Saint Paul says, 'putting on Christ' to radiate him effectively." The particular charism and role of the consecrated teaching Brother was the spiritual life centred on Christ, and "the first effect of faith is to attach us strongly to the knowledge, love and imitation of Jesus Christ, and to union with him." John stipulated in the Rule that ecclesiastics would not be members, the Brothers would not aspire to the priesthood or clerical functions, and there would be no difference between their state and that of their pupils.

Vaugirard – new turning point

On 21st November 1691, the Feast of the Presentation of the Virgin Mary, John and two Brothers, Gabriel Drolin and Nicholas Vuyart, vowed to work for the "complete establishment of the Society of the Christian Schools … without withdrawing from this obligation even if only we three remained and had to beg for alms and live on bread alone." This was not the end of problems but their heroism marked a turning point. A few weeks later, John returned to Reims to resolve, with characteristic sensitivity, a leadership problem that had arisen in the community, now of twenty-seven members. Anxiety about the unknown, the tiring journey, the unrelenting demands of work that increasingly called for classroom teaching, and his own austerity of life left him exhausted, and he realised that they all needed a place where they could recuperate during school holidays. He raised the money to buy a house at Vaugirard on the outskirts of Paris where they could spend a week in spiritual retreat, and gather their strength for the next term. This property also became the location of the first Novitiate that he directed himself for a few years.

Ten years had passed since the Brothers had taken the annual vow of obedience. John decided that it was the right time for some to be given the opportunity to make a lifetime commitment. At Vaugirard on Trinity Sunday

1694, he and twelve disciples made perpetual vows of poverty, chastity, obedience, stability in the Institute, and to teach the poor gratuitously, and the Institute received its unique and irrevocable identity. He continued as Director of Novices, preparing them for the service of God, developing their spirit of faith and sense of vocation, helping them to become good teachers, and strengthen their souls with prayer and spiritual reading. For them he finalised his *Method of Mental Prayer* that owed much to the Sulpician experience and which he adapted to their particular vocation.

His Spirituality and Method

In consultation with the Brothers, John continued to formulate the Rule suited to the circumstances of their active apostolate, yet rooted in the monastic traditions of community life and prayer, silence, self denial, and obedience to the Superior as God's representative. It was to be their means of personal holiness through serving the poor and extending God's kingdom. A Chapter of the Rule is devoted to the Spirit of Faith, the Institute's essential characteristic that helps each member understand that "his vocation is to exercise one of the most important and necessary ministries in the Church that the Apostles of Jesus himself exercised ... In the Spirit of Faith is accomplished that which seems impossible to human eyes."

Spirit of faith

In John's eyes, the Spirit of Faith reverses the disadvantages resulting from original sin by an accurate appreciation of intentions, actions, and attendant circumstances. "It enables those who possess it to look upon everything with the eyes of faith, to do everything with God in view, and attribute to him all that happens. It keeps attention fixed on God, makes him the principle and end of all our actions, and accepts everything as coming from his hand, for 'the Lord gave and the Lord has taken away; blessed be the name of the Lord' ... It is a Spirit that is regulated and guided in all things by the maxims and sentiment of faith based especially on Holy Scripture. We can look on the external appearance of created things with the eyes of the flesh, or with the eyes of nature according to our likes and dislikes, but with this Spirit we can look in accordance with the teaching of faith, and think of created things as God knows them and as faith requires. To live by faith is to make it the rule and principle of one's conduct, actions, and sentiments, to take it as a guide in one's plans, projects, enterprises, and difficulties; to judge and decide everything through a motive of faith and Christian reason ... A soul that is penetrated with sentiments of faith is so raised up to God that it knows nothing and has no taste for anything but God. It applies itself only to God because, being enlightened supernaturally, it places little value on the things of this world."

It was with this faith that John answered God's call to bring the Gospel to children, even if this took him down some uninviting paths. He was certain that Divine Providence would sustain every enterprise because he saw himself merely as God's chosen instrument. Accepting God's will in the Spirit of Faith would be the

foundation and principle feature of his Brothers'
spirituality. He asked them to "do nothing through natural
impulse or from human motive, but do everything for
God's glory and to please him with the help of the Holy
Spirit." He inspired them "never to despair when teaching
seems hard and unproductive, and pupils unresponsive.
Look forward in faith to the heaven that awaits you and
your pupils. What mutual rejoicing there will be, what
union of souls in God's presence, what boundless
celebration you will share knowing 'the glorious
inheritance God has promised the saints' (*Ep* 1:18)".

The source of strength

Above all things, John was devoted to Jesus who alone
knew the Father in the perfect relationship of filial love
that he expressed through humble and perfect obedience
to his Father's will. John accepted our Lord's invitation to
share in that same relationship in which we can know,
love, and serve God. In the Spirit of Faith, he followed
Father Olier's counsel: "To be a good Christian we must
participate in the mysteries of Jesus Christ, our admirable
Saviour who performed them in his person so that they
are the source of abundant graces to the Church." He
implored his Brothers to cooperate with Our Lord in the
divine task of completing his mysteries in us, and
recommended the practice of uniting themselves, their
prayers, work, relaxation, and assistance at Holy Mass "to

the merits and disposition of Jesus, the victim immolated
for the glory of the Father." Likewise, he asked them to
lead their pupils "in uniting their actions to those of Our
Lord so that, sanctified by his merits, what they do will
be agreeable to God and a means of salvation."

Most Blessed Virgin

When the world turned against him, John accepted even
betrayal and persecution as God's permissive will, and
turned to his Saviour with confidence, remembering
always the divine infant who teaches innocence, reliance
upon God, and self-sacrifice. He found strength in the
devotions to which he was ever faithful, and the love of
which became the hallmark of his Institute. He honoured
the Mother of God, "the fullness of grace who tenderly
loves all humanity - the children for whose salvation she
longs." He corrected those who omitted "Most" from her
title of Most Blessed Virgin gently asking, "Please call
her 'Most Blessed'. She fully deserves it". He asked the
Brothers to "Have great devotion to the Most Blessed
Virgin because God himself honours her in a special way.
He has raised her above all pure creatures because she
carried in her womb the Son who is equal to himself and
has his identical nature." He enthroned her as the
Superioress of the Institute that has always celebrated her
feasts with the reverence and honour that is her due. He
loved her Rosary because "the Lord's Prayer and the Hail

Mary, having the highest authorisation of the Church, cannot be surpassed in holiness", and the Rosary of the De La Salle Brothers has an additional sixth decade primarily in honour of her Immaculate Conception.

The Sacred Hearts of Jesus and Mary were particularly dear to him: "Let us honour these two hearts which are so intimately united; let us go to God the Father through the Heart of Jesus; let us go to our Saviour through the Heart of Mary ... We shall obtain everything from the Father and the Holy Spirit through the Heart of Jesus, and everything from the Son through the Heart of Mary." He had great confidence in her spouse, the great Saint Joseph who was foster-father of the divine child. He placed the Institute under his patronage and protection, and asked the Brothers to "recite his litany every day to receive his spirit as guardian of the child Jesus."

The saints

Never forgotten were Saint Michael and the Guardian Angels, Saints Peter and Paul and the Four Evangelists, Saint John the Baptist, Saint Cassian whose zeal as an educator won him the crown of martyrdom and, indeed, all the saints as individual persons to be honoured. "It is good to ask the saints to pray for us and look kindly on us. When they were alive, they had compassion on sinners and prayed to God for them. Now, they have even a greater feeling of pity for us fellow humans, because they have before their eyes him who is the source of all mercy. Now, they are more aware of our weakness than when they were alive and their charity, far from diminishing, has greatly increased."

He venerated the founders of religious orders who were so dedicated to the glory of God like Saint Benedict whose Rule and monastic tradition guided his own foundation, Saints Dominic, Ignatius of Loyola, Philip Neri, and Teresa of Avila. He asked Saints Francis Xavier, Charles Borromeo and Francis de Sales to let him share their spirit in directing souls to God with gentleness, and help him emulate their apostolic zeal, dauntless bravery and self-denial. They answered his prayers in abundance.

Word of God

In an age when individuals were not encouraged to read Holy Scripture, John wanted the Bothers to be absorbed in God's word, always have a copy of the New Testament with them, read from it every day, and share it with their pupils. "He has entrusted you with the message of reconciliation. Appeal to children as if God were appealing through you, for you have been destined to cultivate these young plants by announcing the Gospel to them. See them as the children of God Himself." His vision was born of love and faith, and motivated his Brothers. It was certainly a challenge when facing a few dozen assorted youngsters from the poor quarters of

Paris, but they were not found wanting. Standards of living and morality in the capital left much to be desired but the Brothers, motivated by zeal for the salvation of souls were determined to protect children from contamination. They themselves took John's advice: "Some contact with the world is inevitable, but be reserved so as not to be harmed. It is hard to preserve innocence of heart, so let us thank God that we have withdrawn from the world."

'The Conduct of Schools'

John's masterpiece of 1695 is hailed as an educational milestone that anticipates all that is best in teaching method and classroom management. As a treatise on education's fundamental principles, it reflects the momentous achievement of his ideals, practical common sense, and religious approach to the nurture of minds and hearts. The distinguished inspector of schools and poet, Matthew Arnold, paid tribute to its timeless wisdom, relevance, and applicability as an educational classic: "Later works on the same subject have scarcely improved on its precepts and have none of its religious feeling."

John had witnessed children without hope for the future, living in a sub-culture of poverty, ignorance, violence, crime and in many cases, fatherless. Blain described "homes where they saw nothing but bad example, heard nothing but bad language and were left in complete ignorance. Parents abandoned them to their natural inclinations and protected them from correction, so they imagined they could do what they please at school, even in church, with impunity. People deplored the situation but did nothing for fear of abuse from infuriated and ill-mannered parents, and looked to the Brothers to put things right."

John's antidote was to inspire the teacher with "a father's love for his pupils, ready to devote time and energy to them, as concerned to save them from wickedness as to dispel ignorance." Pupils were reminded of the importance of their religion by the pictures in the classroom, the catechism and religious instruction, the text books used, the religious habit of their teachers, and by the encouragement they received first thing every morning to work with religious motive. John identified the "hidden curriculum" of attitudes, values, and experiences in the transmission of knowledge and skills from teacher to taught that creates the ethos of the authentic Christian school. He was prescient in his recognition of the essential exercise of parental responsibility, and the injustice of letting a disruptive minority threaten the well being of the cooperative majority.

Behaviour and the classroom

"A quiet classroom atmosphere saves time otherwise lost correcting misbehaviour. More progress is made, and satisfaction in achievement makes work less burdensome. Silence is one of the principle means of maintaining order in schools. For this reason, every teacher will see that it is kept in class, as much by example as by words."

"Teachers will be careful to keep a modest and serious demeanour, not of severity or anger, but reserved in what they do and say. They must not become familiar with their pupils, nor allow them to speak to them other than with respect."

"We must be both gentle and firm towards those entrusted to our care, and act with great patience without letting children aspire to impunity. Gentleness consists in never allowing harshness, anger or passion to appear in a reprimand, but in showing a father's gravity and tender compassion."

"Sometimes pupils must be sent away from school but only on the advice of the headmaster. These are the dissolute who harm others, truants, and those who have been regularly corrected but refuse to mend their behaviour."

"Some parents pay little attention to the conduct of their children who do exactly what they please, have no respect for their parents, are disobedient, and grumble at the least thing. Sometimes, these faults do not come from an evil disposition, but from having been left to themselves ... Some parents give their children everything they demand, and never correct them."

Teaching a class

John's fundamental advice, now taken for granted, supported the innovations of the simultaneous method of teaching in the vernacular:

"Determine the relative intelligence of every pupil in the class;

prepare every lesson thoroughly;

adapt language and explanation to class ability, and do not neglect slower pupils;

speak sensibly, clearly and precisely in correct language;

make sure the meaning of words used is understood;

use accurate definitions;

make sure you know the facts and the truth of what you say;

use the system of question and answer;

ask questions that provoke explanations;

help the pupil use his power of thought, form judgements, and seek answers himself;

make sure pupils understand the basics of a subject before moving to advanced work;

introduce few principles at a time and explain them carefully;

progress from the simple to the complex, the easy to the difficult;

speak to the eyes of the class by using the blackboard;
do not expose the pupils to false models and standards."

Supplements to 'The Conduct of Schools'

John wrote text books for every subject, and *The Duties of a Christian* – a masterly exposition of the Faith he wanted to share with children – was so influential that it ran to two hundred and fifty editions. His *Rules of Christian Behaviour and Politeness* covered appearance, deportment, dress, table manners, and decent behaviour in everyday, social routines. His *Exercises of Piety for use in the Christian Schools* included recommendations of personal performance review, and progress projection that anticipated modern practices of self-assessment, evaluation and forward planning.

John did not want young people to abandon school to pursue an alternative "education" on the streets, so he founded a religious order and pioneered schools that enabled them to grow, develop, and fulfil their destiny. He offered his Brothers personal guidance in his *Meditations for the Sundays, Major Feasts, and Time of Retreat.* These link the principles of the spiritual life to those of enlightened pedagogy, and apply the appropriate Gospel passages to the teaching profession and the religious life. As always, his language is simple, direct, and heartfelt, and reveals the greatness of a man achieving holiness through deep religious conviction with charity overflowing from his love of God.

Makings of a good teacher

"Turn over in your mind the words of Saint Paul, that God appointed in the Church, apostles, prophets and teachers, and you will be persuaded that he has placed you in your work as well ... the Holy Spirit is manifested in each of these gifts for the common good, that is the good of the Church."

"The grace that has been given to you to teach children, to announce the Gospel to them, and instil in them the spirit of religion, is a great gift of God who has called you to this holy service. Have a great esteem for their Christian education because it is a powerful means of making them true children of God and citizens of heaven."

"It often happens that those occupations which people undervalue, produce more fruit than the most brilliant. You should regard your occupation as one of the most important and the most excellent in the Church, for it is one most suited to sustain it and give it a solid foundation."

"In everything you do as teachers, let the children entrusted to your care see you as the servants of God as you go about your work with genuine love and real diligence. What commits you even more to your work is that you are not only ministers of God, but also of Jesus

Christ and the Church. Let them be moved by your hard-working perseverance, and let them feel as though God were exhorting them through you, since you are ambassadors for Christ."

"Parents often allow children to be on their own, to roam around as if they had no home ... They do not send their children to school ... perhaps because they have to work and leave them to fend for themselves. Accustomed to an idle life, these young people find it difficult to go to work and, through association with unsuitable company, fall into immorality and lawlessness ... There is holy anger, prompted by zeal, which moves us to reprove with warmth those whom our mildness failed to correct."

"Show by your zeal that you love those whom God has handed over to you, just as Christ loves the Church. Make sure that the children are built into the structure of the house of God. Work so that the riches of God's grace that he has given them, may be made manifest to succeeding generations. He extends his help in his teaching, and to you when you teach and educate them, so that they may receive their inheritance in the Kingdom of God and of Jesus Christ Our Lord."

Progress at a Price

In 1698, with financial help from the latest parish priest of
Saint-Sulpice, Father de la Chetardye, and a benefactress,
John relocated the Novitiate from Vaugirard to larger
accommodation known as Grand' Maison. He dedicated the
chapel there to Saint Cassian, a teacher-martyr of the early
Church, appointed a Director of Novices (now numbering
thirty five) an Inspector of Schools, a bursar, a secretary, and
an infirmarian. He also opened a school for poor children in
an annex to the house that provided teacher-training
opportunities in an early example of what became known as
a "Demonstration School". A further innovation was the
establishment of a "Christian Academy" that provided a
religious, technical, and practical education on Sundays for
young men in Saint-Sulpice who, of necessity, had to work
on the other six days of the week. Soon, five schools in Paris
were educating a thousand pupils, and others were opened in
Avignon, Troyes, Marseilles, Moulins, Boulogne, Calais,
Dijon, Provence and Languedoc.

School in Rome

John was devoted to the Church of Rome and to Saint
Peter's successor who was now Pope Clement XI. He

urged the Brothers, "Above all things, have an entire submission to the Church, especially in these troubled times, and never be separated from her authority." In 1701, he decided to open a school in Rome as the first step in seeking the Holy See's approval of the Institute, and "to ask God the grace that it should always be submissive to the Church." He entrusted this important enterprise to the outstanding Brother Gabriel Drolin who, it will be remembered, had joined him and Brother Nicholas Vuyart in the heroic vow of perseverance ten years earlier.

Not only did Gabriel succeed but, because of the unavailability of personnel, he ran the establishment on his own for twenty seven years. John's frequent letters of support over the years are touching reminders of his loving kindness towards all his Brethren, and his humility. In one he wrote, "I do not wish to put myself forward in anything and I shall not do so in Rome any more than elsewhere. Providence makes the first step and I am happy to act as it dictates. When I act independently, I do not expect good results, nor does God usually give his blessing."

Universal esteem

James II of England tried to recover his throne from William III of Orange but was defeated at the Battle of the Boyne on 12th July 1690. Louis XIV offered him shelter in Paris and approached Cardinal de Noailles for help with the education of children whose parents had followed their king into exile. The Cardinal immediately turned to John who, with another Brother, undertook the teaching of fifty children at Grand' Maison. When King James visited the classes, he expressed his admiration and gratitude.

The Devil at work

The following year, the previously cooperative Father de la Chetardye thought he should be the Superior of the Brothers in his parish, wanted the Novices to serve Mass in clerical cassock and cotta, and forwarded the view that Brothers everywhere should be directed by the parish priest. In John's absence visiting a school in Chartres, he listened to complaints from some unhappy postulants about alleged harsh treatment from Brother Michael the Novice Master. He eagerly reported this to Cardinal de Noailles who tried to appoint a Father Bricot as head of the Institute. John, who saw the will of God in all things, was humbly prepared to accept this deposition, but the Brothers would not hear of it and threatened to leave Paris altogether. Their determination halted the manoeuvres but relationships did not fully recover. Despite every effort on his part, John suffered the pain of losing the friendship and support of two fellow priests.

The 'Writing Masters'

Attacks now came from another quarter. The private "Little Schools" mentioned earlier taught reading, but not the handwriting skills that were the prerogative of the "Writing Masters". They were outraged that the Brothers included handwriting in their curriculum and that fees were not charged even when they could be afforded. They mounted an assault and incited the gendarmes to descend on one of the schools. Books, furniture, and equipment were confiscated and the Brothers summoned to appear in court where they lost their case, and were forbidden to operate further without royal permission.

Betrayal

The school that gave opportunities for teacher training was directed by Brother Nicholas Vuyart, one of John's early and trusted disciples. The priest who had been financing the establishment died and left Nicholas a legacy for its continued maintenance. It came as a terrible blow when, carried away by success, Nicholas abandoned his vocation, and tried to run the school on his own. John found no consolation when the school collapsed, but the Writing Masters were delighted. They continued their campaign of harassment, and Father de la Chetardye, who could have effected a reconciliation, did nothing. Some years later, Nicholas Vuyart repented and sought readmission to the Institute. John, ever compassionate, would have welcomed him back, but the Brothers would not agree.

Perseverance

In spite of everything, John never wavered, nor was he deterred from responding to the needs of young people. In expanding the work of the Institute, he accepted every new trial as a fresh opportunity offered by God. In 1705, when King Louis wanted serving seamen, naval officers, and pilots in the ports to add theoretical knowledge to their practical experience, he opened a nautical school in Calais that received financial help by royal decree. At the same time, requests came from Dijon to have a school there, and from Rouen to take charge of two charity schools and add two more in due course.

Move to St Yon

In contrast to the negative atmosphere in Paris, things were going so well in Rouen that John decided to transfer the Institute's headquarters to this capital of Normandy. He rented a large property in the suburbs of St Yon that became the Institute's Mother House, including the Novitiate, for most of the following century. As soon as the Brothers left Paris, John's momentous achievement was fully appreciated. Father de la Chetardye's attempts to run the schools were chaotic and he was besieged by crowds of parents demanding the Brothers' return. He wrote to John begging his help, and promising to resolve the issue with the Writing Masters. Without a trace of bitterness, John sent twelve Brothers back to Saint-Sulpice, ten to teach, one to keep house, and one to be Inspector of Schools. They were welcomed with affection and enthusiasm, and the parish priest showed grateful admiration, but his attitude towards John never became cordial, perhaps because he was in awe of his qualities.

Early 'technical' and 'approved' schools

The merchant classes in Rouen wanted their sons to have an education more advanced than the elementary syllabus or the customary classical direction. They preferred a modern practical content adapted to future careers in business and commerce. To meet their requirements, John opened a boarding school in the grounds of St Yon with a syllabus that prepared the way for the Technical School of the "tri-partite system" envisaged in the 1944 Education Act three centuries later. He also opened a reformatory for young delinquents, the humane and positive programme of which brought remarkable results and was the forerunner of the Home Office Approved Schools later directed by the Brothers that won such approbation from the secular authorities.

The ambience and facilities of St Yon made it an ideal location for all the Brothers to come for rest and retreat. Endeavours were blessed with more postulants and novices whom John placed in the care of Brother Barthelemy, a devoted and gifted religious. He saw that the expanding

Institute needed revised administration, and appointed two Brothers "Visitor", for the north and south of France, to support the communities. He continued to make his own visits as much as possible, and wrote many letters to his Brothers, with sensitive understanding of the enormity of their task, comforting, encouraging, guiding them with his unique spiritual wisdom and perception of education.

Visitations

The animosity of Church leaders in Paris towards John persisted, and he thought it better to absent himself so as not to jeopardise the Brothers' work. He set out to visit the schools in the south via Avignon where he opened another one, continued through the dangerous Huguenot territory of Alès and Les Vins where the Brothers had been physically attacked, and on to Mendé where the community was directed by Brother Timothy. When he arrived in Marseilles, he was overjoyed to find the schools and community flourishing, and he decided to open a Novitiate here for this southern province that was such a distance from St Yon. He wrote to Brother Gabriel, still on his own in Rome after eleven years, telling him that "it will be difficult to send you a Brother before I open a Novitiate here." Four months later, he informed him that this had happened, and that he hoped to see his loyal disciple soon and visit St Peter's tomb. Sadly, this was not to be.

The Final Years

Marseilles was a hotbed of Jansenism that was embraced by clergy resentful of Papal denunciations. They tried to win John to their cause and persuade him to introduce their doctrine in the schools, but he left them in no doubt about his orthodoxy, obedience to the Holy See, and disapproval of their error. Whereas they had been welcoming and supportive, they now ostracised him and even subverted some of the Brothers. One school closed and, in such a tense situation, vocations were not forthcoming. For the sake of the Brothers he decided to depart, and left Brother Timothy in charge of the Novitiate and the one remaining school.

The pain of self-doubt

A dark night of the soul descended upon John whose confidence was so undermined that he wondered if he had ever been doing the right thing. In spiritual perplexity, he sought God's guidance and trudged thirty miles to La Sainte Baume where Saint Mary Magdalene was reported to have ended her days. His enemies accused him of abandoning his mission in despair, and he was particularly disappointed that his hope of linking schools in southern France with Rome had been crushed. Like his adored Master, he spent forty days in prayer and solitude before going to Mendé. What grief it must have been for him that the Brothers' community, thinking his mismanagement had caused the problems in Marseilles, gave him such a cold reception that he took refuge in the town's Capuchin priory. Then, Brother Timothy arrived to tell him that the Marseilles Novitiate had closed, news that again he humbly accepted as God's will. Despite personal heartache, he still managed to restore confidence and relationships in the Mendé community.

Grenoble and encouragement

John spent a few days in retreat with the Carthusians at La Grande Chartreuse on his way to Grenoble where he stayed ten months with the community. It seems a long time to be away from the Institute's headquarters, but he was preparing the Brothers to take responsibility for schools and communities without his presence. Naturally, he stayed in touch by letter, and regularly sent Brothers to Paris and elsewhere to report on progress while he took their classes. It was now 1713, he was sixty two, suffering from asthma and rheumatism, and his general health affected by ceaseless labour and self-denial. This did not stop him accepting an invitation from a priest friend to visit the mountain shrine of Our Lady at Parménie that was also the home of Sister Louise, a saintly recluse famed for the sound advice she gave to those plagued by uncertainty and doubt. When he shared his misgivings with her, he was wonderfully relieved by her unhesitating direction that he must continue the work that God so obviously wanted him to do.

As if to confirm what Louise had said, kindly Providence gave him further reassurance. At Parmenie, he met a soldier of noble birth recuperating from a wound received at the battle of Malplaquet. He now wanted to dedicate his life to God's service and had made initial overtures to the Trappists and Carthusians but, in conversation with John, was inspired by what he heard about the Brothers' apostolate. He went to Grenoble to spend some time with the community, after which he asked to be admitted into the Institute. When John joyfully clothed him with the religious habit, he received the name Brother Irenée, and would later become Novice Master at St Yon where, for thirty years, he faithfully upheld the traditions of the holy founder.

Relocating the Novitiate

Meanwhile in John's absence, parish priests in Paris renewed efforts to control the Institute and change rules to suit themselves. Bearing in mind their vow of obedience "to the Superiors and the body of the Society" which John himself had professed, the Brothers wrote to their "very dear Father" commanding him, in obedience, to resume general management. It was with confidence restored that John accepted this as God's wish. He left Grenoble for Paris in 1715, visited the Dijon community *en route* and, after an absence of more than two years, arrived to the Brothers' enthusiastic welcome. His first words are cherished in the Institute as a measure of his humble simplicity. "Here I am. What do you want me to do?" Four years earlier during a famine, he had transferred the Novitiate from St Yon to the capital. Now he relocated it back to Rouen where the rural seclusion was more compatible with the Novices' religious development. With inimitable tact and charity, he restored normality in Paris, and returned to St Yon hoping to prepare for life's end in prayerful tranquillity.

First Superior General

Though only sixty-five, John was worn out by constant effort, unrelenting demands, and suffering from rheumatism and asthma. Only once did he leave St Yon when, in 1716, he was invited to visit the schools in Boulogne and Calais. Their success, the heart-warming reception given by his Brothers, and the gratitude of the citizens brought much comfort. He felt the time had now come for a new Superior, so planned to convene the Institute's first General Chapter to elect a candidate and decide measures for future growth. He commissioned Brother Barthelemy to visit the hundred and twenty

Brothers in the twenty-one communities throughout France, inform them what was intended, and secure their support for the decision-making Chapter. Brother Gabriel in Rome was not forgotten and was consulted through correspondence. Barthelemy's assignment admittedly took five months, but gave him opportunity to assess schools and communities and identify topics for discussion.

With confidence in the Holy Spirit, the Brother Directors of the sixteen principal communities assembled in Chapter at St Yon on Pentecost Sunday, 16th May 1717. Their holy founder led them in a short retreat and, two days later, Brother Barthelemy was unanimously elected Superior much to John's delight. The assembly then examined and discussed the 1695 draft Rule in the light of experience, practice and development, and submitted their recommendations to John. He agreed to use them in drawing up the definitive version, but emphasised that the direction of the Institute was now in the hands of their new Superior General.

Praying and teaching

A few months later, he received an unexpected legacy that enabled him to complete the purchase of the Mother House at St Yon. He finished the revision of the Rule, completed his treatise *The Method of Mental Prayer* to which he attached prime importance, and added further gems to the sublime *Meditations* bequeathed to his

Brothers for their spiritual sustenance. He spent many hours in prayer, but found the time to go to the schoolyard and chat to the youngsters who warmed to his personality and responded happily to his obviously genuine interest and pleasure in their company. Having preached obedience all his life, he gently declined requests to visit or open schools, and referred correspondence to his Brother Superior whose permission he always sought even in minor matters.

Last illness

John continued to teach the boarders and Novices, and was at his happiest living as "the least worthy member of the community", but the Devil made a last, futile assault. The parish priest of St Yon demanded that the Brothers and the boarders should attend Sunday Mass in his church. It was respectfully pointed out that this would be inappropriate because of the pupil boarders who had behavioural problems, but he complained to the Archbishop of Rouen, another envious and ill-informed prelate, who forbade John to celebrate Mass for the Brothers or hear their Confessions. This final trial towards the end of his journey was faced with his habitual reaction to pain and disappointment, "God be blessed!".

In January 1719, his health swiftly deteriorated, and severe, frequent headaches brought on by an accident joined the rheumatism and asthma. On Ash Wednesday, he wanted to begin his strict Lenten fast until Brother Barthelemy and his Father-confessor forbade it, and a visit from the doctor confirmed the seriousness of his condition. He managed to celebrate Mass for the last time on 19th March, the feast of Saint Joseph to whose patronage he had entrusted his Institute.

To Paradise

On Maundy Thursday it was arranged that John should receive the Last Sacraments. He asked to be dressed in his priestly vestments and, with great effort, fell to his knees when the bell announced the approach of the Blessed Sacrament. Afterwards he talked to his Brothers, encouraging them to preserve and love their vocation by avoiding worldly attitudes and values, and by being faithful to their Rule. In the early hours of Good Friday, 7th April 1719, he recited his favourite prayer to Our Lady: "Mary, loving Mother, protect us from the enemy and receive us at the hour of our death." His last words were, "I adore in all things the will of God in my regard," then breathed his last to join the Divine Master whose cross he had shared and whom he had served so nobly.

When the news of John's death was heard, all France mourned and there was a remarkable outpouring of grief in Rouen. Prelates, clergy, members of religious orders and crowds of the laity flocked to St Yon, and reverently moved through the chapel where his body lay in his priestly vestments, some yielding to the impulse to cut a fragment of clothing, even hair, to keep as a precious relic. He was buried with liturgical dignity in the parish church of Saint Sever - the sixth century bishop who, by happy chance was also a great teacher, writer and philosopher. The congregation at the Requiem Mass, arranged after Easter Sunday, were consoled by a joyous sense of celebration in achievement.

From heaven, John watched over his Institute and it expanded rapidly from the existing foundations throughout France and in Rome. In 1725, Pope Benedict XIII granted the Brothers of the Christian Schools the most solemn form of recognition with the Bull of Approbation as a Papal Order rather than diocesan, and King Louis XV confirmed royal and legal status with letters patent. Because they had opened schools and communities in Switzerland, the Brothers survived the French Revolution's exterminations and returned to France when more favourable conditions arrived with Napoleon.

Devotion to John Baptist De La Salle

Brother Barthelemy survived John by only a year and, despite diocesan attempts to impose a priest as Superior General, the Brothers succeeded in electing the virtuous and capable Brother Timothy who would lead the Institute for thirty years until 1750. His first endeavour was to build a chapel at St Yon worthy of the Mother House and John, and arranged the transfer of his remains from the parish church. He invited Canon Blain, now chaplain at St Yon, to write the two volume biography that would assist the cause of canonisation. This definitive work was completed, but the process was impeded by the unhappy socio-political circumstances in France that culminated in the Revolution.

The sincerest sign of devotion and appreciation of accomplishment is a determination to emulate. Many religious congregations have been permeated by John's spirit that has formed their special character and inspired their Rules. They include the Institute of the Christian Schools of Mercy (Saint Mary Magdalene Postel), the Brothers of Saint Gabriel (St Grignion de Montfort), the Christian Brothers of Ireland, and The Brothers of Mercy. Another admirer was Saint John Bosco who, in 1859, founded the Society of Saint Francis de Sales, a community of priests dedicated to the education of boys and young men.

John was beatified by Pope Leo XIII in 1888 and
canonised two years later. His feast entered the Roman
Calendar on 15th May but, since its reordering in 1969, is
now 7th April, the anniversary of his death. The Institute
additionally continues to celebrate 15th May. John never
realised his dream of visiting Rome but, in 1938, his
mortal remains, resting in Lembecq-les-Hal in Belgium,
were translated in triumphal procession to the new
Mother House of the Institute on Rome's via Aurelia and
the "Roman Priest" had come home. The feast of the
translation is 26th January, and on 17th November, the
Brothers celebrate the feast of the Dedication of the
Roman church of Saint John Baptist De La Salle.

From the Liturgy

"Suffer the little children to come unto me, and forbid
them not, for of such is the Kingdom of Heaven".
Entrance Antiphon.

"Lord, for the Christian education of the poor and the
safeguarding of youth in the way of salvation, you raised
up Saint John Baptist and, through him, formed a new
religious family in the Church. Through his intercession
and example, may we be inspired with zeal for your glory
in saving souls, and come to share his crown in Heaven.

Father, you chose Saint John Baptist De La Salle to
give young people a Christian education. Give your
Church teachers who will devote themselves to help your

children grow as Christian men and women". *Prayer of the Church*.

"The disciples came to Jesus and said, 'Who is the greatest in the Kingdom of heaven?' So He called a little child to Him and set the child in front of them. Then He said, 'I tell you solemnly, unless you change and become like little children, you will never enter the Kingdom of Heaven. And so, the one who makes himself as little as this little child is the greatest in the Kingdom of Heaven. Anyone who welcomes a little child in my name welcomes me'". (*Mt* 18:1-5).

Patron of all teachers

In the Holy Year of 1950, just a few months before the tercentenary of his birth, Pope Pius XII declared Saint John Baptist De La Salle the Patron of all teachers. Around this time there had been justifiable speculation that he might be elevated to the ranks of the Doctors of the Church. That this was not to be detracts nothing from the inspirational quality, breadth, and orthodoxy of his prolific writings. In 1955, a solemn High Mass was celebrated in Westminster Cathedral by Cardinals, the Archbishops and Bishops of England and Wales and many others, to mark the centenary of the Brothers' first arrival in England at Clapham in 1855. For this occasion, an older hymn was newly translated by Monsignor Ronald Knox and set to music by R.Dom A.Gregory Murray of Downside Abbey.

Of Blessed John that gave to Thee
All of himself, Thy own to be,
His heart, his mind, his arduous days,
Jesus to Thee we sing the praise.

Blest Fountain-head, secure Retreat,
Where holiness and wisdom meet!
By love, the only spell he knew,
To Thee his little ones he drew.

Softly as dew on grass it fell
On children's hearts, his gracious spell;
Heaven's rugged pathway to their eyes,
Seemed like a flowering paradise.

Now that the heavenly light he shares
With angels, may those loving prayers
Still to his sons an influence lend,
The hopes of childhood still befriend.

Praise to the Father, praise to Thee;
Jesus, and to the Spirit be;
Grant us amid Thy saints to rest
With Thy beholding ever blessed.

A living legacy

Saint John Baptist De La Salle offered his disciples a way
of life that leads to heroic sanctity. Among those the
Church has raised to the honours of the altar are Saints
Benildus, Mutien-Marie, Miguel, and Jamie Hilario, the

most recent of whom was canonised by Pope John Paul II in 1999. Blessed Brothers Solomon, Leon, Roger, and Uldaric were martyred during the French Revolution, and their compatriots Brothers Arnold and Scubilion have also been beatified. The beatified Brothers martyred in Spain between 1934 and 1936 include eight from Asturias, and nine from Almeria, and no fewer than sixty-three other blessed martyrs from the communities of Catalunya, Santa Cruz de Mudela, Consuegra, Lorca and Valencia. The causes of other Brothers continue to be promoted, and the beatification of Raphael Rafringa, the first Brother from Madagascar is scheduled for early 2009.

Today, the De La Salle Brothers remain one of the largest teaching Orders in the Church. They continue their mission in eighty countries of the world, in primary and secondary schools, teacher training colleges, universities, and in their extended apostolate of evangelisation and proclamation of the Faith, educational renewal, supporting the rights of children, and exercising a beneficent presence in multi-religious societies. They have extended their work to related ministries that include residential courses in education and spiritual development, family counselling, refugee support, writing and publishing, campus chaplaincy, and parish and diocesan endeavours.

Vincent de Paul

Amid the wars and turmoil of 16th-century Reformation France, and in the midst of great suffering and poverty, Providence provided an amazing example of apostolic zeal. Highly intelligent, physically small, and burning with love for Christ in the poor, Vincent de Paul stimulated a major change in the social consciousness of France and far beyond. His Religious Orders for men and women continue today. This account of his life and times captures the amazing spirit of this humble and courageous man, who truly loved and served the poor.

Barry Midgley, a retired Headmaster, has spent most of his professional life in Catholic education. He has published several titles with CTS and lives in East Anglia.

ISBN: 978 1 86082 503

CTS Code: B 701

John Vianney

For over 40 years John Vianney was the parish priest of Ars, near Lyons, France. From modest farming stock and poor at his studies, he overcame many obstacles to become a priest, and to care for his neglected flock. His holiness, preaching and sanctity drew endless numbers of pilgrims. His fame in his own lifetime matched that of a modern day Mother Teresa or Padre Pio. This highly informative booklet reveals the real person behind the famous Curé d'Ars, and his boundless love for Christ.

Barry Midgley, a retired Headmaster, has spent most of his professional life in Catholic education. He has published several titles with CTS and lives in East Anglia.

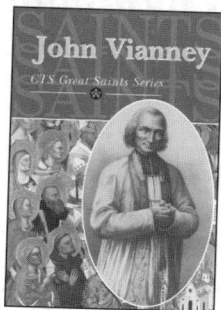

ISBN: 978 1 86082 478 4

CTS Code: B 698